BY SHAWNISE BEATTY
Illustrated by Alejandra Osuna

This is a work of fiction. Names, characters, places, and incidents either are the product of the author's imagination or are used fictitiously. Any resemblance to actual persons, living or dead, events, or locales is entirely coincidental.

Copyright © 2018 by Shawnise N. Beatty
All rights reserved. No part of this book may be reproduced or used in any manner without written permission of the copyright owner except for the use of quotations in a book review. For more information, address: beatty1233@gmail.com

First paperback edition November 2018

Written by Shawnise Beatty

Illustrated by Alejandra Osuna

Book design by Kimberly Peticolas

Editing by Naomi Eagleson

ISBN 9781727838084 (paperback)

To my loving parents, Priscilla Ann Miller and Stephen Lamont Beatty.
I love you both and miss you dearly.
Please keep watching over me and guiding me in the light.
Thank you to my dear Aunts, Malika and Gina, you are my lifelines.

Priscilla lay in her bed looking at the stars in the sky. She would be starting her first day of K1 tomorrow. She felt angry and sad because her mom and dad had died when she was a baby. Priscilla wished she had a regular family with a mother and father, like every other kid at school.

Priscilla lived with her Auntie Ann. She took Priscilla in after her parents died in a car accident. Auntie Ann had been taking care of Priscilla since she was a baby. Auntie Ann did not have any children of her own.

Auntie Ann said, "Good night. I love you, my dear."

"Good night, Auntie Ann!" Priscilla yelled back. She held her teddy tight. "Teddy, please make tomorrow a great first day," she said as she closed her eyes. Then she fell fast asleep.

"Good morning, my love muffin," Auntie Ann said as she kissed Priscilla on the forehead.

"Good morning, Auntie Ann," Priscilla said as she stretched and looked at the bright sun shining in.

Priscilla quickly did the morning routine Auntie Ann had taught her. She jumped up and down on her bed and screamed:

"I AM ALIVE, I AM LOVE, and I AM READY FOR THE WORLD."

Priscilla took a shower, got dressed, brushed her teeth, and ran downstairs to eat her breakfast.

Auntie Ann was making her favorite Mickey Mouse pancakes with strawberry eyes. Auntie Ann said, "Have a great day on your first day of school. You'll meet new friends today and share who you are with your classroom."

As Priscilla finished eating, she said, "I don't have anything to share, Auntie Ann. I'm scared everyone will talk about how they have parents and I don't." Auntie Ann gave Priscilla a big hug. "My dear, love is all you need, and I love you with all my heart." Priscilla loved Auntie Ann so much.

Auntie Ann looked at the clock. "Grab your lunch box. It's time to catch your school bus."

Priscilla smiled as the bus pulled up; its name said "JOY BUS."

The bus arrived at Peace Elementary School. There were many children getting off buses. Teachers were asking each kid for their name as they got off the bus. "Hi, I'm Miss Loveheart. Welcome to kindergarten."

Priscilla walked into her new classroom. Miss Loveheart said, "Welcome to room 143, where we learn and have fun. Please hang up your jackets and put away your lunch."

Miss Loveheart said, "Today, class, we will draw pictures and write a story about one thing you enjoyed this summer or the most exciting fun you had this summer with family or friends."

Priscilla was excited; she loved to draw and write. Then she began to get nervous. What would she write about? Priscilla thought, I will be the only kid without a mom or dad.

Priscilla drew her picture and smiled. It was a picture of her and Auntie Ann at the water park they had visited this past summer. Priscilla was happy about her story and picture; however, she was still scared about what the other kids would think.

Miss Loveheart said, "Who would like to share first?"
Barbara raised her hand. "Pick me, pick me, teacher." Barbara talked all about her new cat, Henry. She said he was her family and best friend. Barbara said that her grandpa gave Henry to her as a gift. "I love Henry. He is special to me. He likes candy, hugs, and kisses." Barbara held up her drawing to show the class.

Lou said, "Me, me, I'm next, teacher." Lou began reading: "The most fun I ever had this summer was at Disney World with my big brother and Mom and Dad."

Then Jill jumped up and started reading, "I loved going fishing all summer long with my dad. I got to wear a life jacket. My dad had me touch a slimy, icky worm. Yuck, it was gross. But it was fun because I got to be with my dad."

Priscilla was feeling very anxious and was sweating, so she screamed out, "I don't have a mom or dad! I live with Auntie Ann." She was holding back her tears so she could look at the class.

Sean yelled, "I have two dads and they love me very much."

It seemed like all the children began yelling left and right.

Carlos yelled, "I live with my grandma and my little brother."

Ryan said, "I live with my big sister and our dog, Rufus."

Kelly screamed out, "I live with my two moms and my baby sister."

The entire class was shouting out the names of their family, cats, dogs, and each person who lived inside their home.

Miss Loveheart put her left hand in the air and her right finger on her lip and stood in silence. Then everyone began to calm down. Miss Loveheart explained to students about the world being very colorful and we all had many different, unique families and that made each of us special. Miss Loveheart said, "Love is all we need."

The day was ending. Miss Loveheart told the class they all had a wonderful first day in K1. Everyone got to take home the pictures they drew of their families.

As Priscilla waited for her school bus to take her home, she couldn't wait to tell Auntie Ann about how great her first day of school was."

Priscilla got on the bus and saw Barbara from her classroom, so she sat next to her. Barbara said, "Hi," and talked all about how much she loved Henry her cat. She hugged her picture and said, "Henry is my best friend."

Priscilla asked Barbara what was so special about Henry the cat. Barbara said, "Henry was a gift from my grandpa before he died, so I love my Henry very much."

Priscilla smiled and said, "I love Henry the cat as well," and gave Barbara a hug.

"Good bye, Barbara. See you tomorrow. Tell Henry I said hi." Priscilla saw Auntie Ann waving for her as she got off the school bus. She ran and gave Auntie Ann a big hug.

"How was your day?" asked Auntie Ann. "Tell me all about it on our walk home."

Priscilla smiled and said Auntie Ann you were right "Love is all we need". I love my bus driver, my teacher Miss Loveheart, and all my friends at school. Priscilla said, "Auntie the world is very colorful and we all have many different unique families and that is what makes each of us special".

The End.

Shawnise Beatty was born and raised in Boston, Massachusetts. Shawnise loves kids and the healing power of telling stories. After growing up in an unconventional family of her own, Shawnise decided to write this book for the children who don't always have both a mother and a father. This is her first book.

Made in the USA
Middletown, DE
10 November 2018